Design by Gabriela Mata

Photography by Paul Council @councilimaging

LOVE & SEASONING
IN TIMES OF QUARANTINE

A culinary journey that connects our experiences and loving with the challenges during the pandemic

Pedro Mata
@pedromatav Pedro Mata Villalba

Photography by Paul Council

PROLOGUE

My love for cooking started since I was a little kid. While participating in the preparation of delicious meals, I received inheritance of family recipes, advice on how to acquire the best ingredients at the market and to combine them in special ways and then share the results with friends and family that I love and miss.

In each stage of my life this motivation to discover new ingredients, taste unique dishes in the places where I have been blessed to travel and incorporate them into my culinary experience, has contributed on this daily growth of my love for cooking. Sharing it with my loved ones has always been the best part by far. It feels amazing when there is nothing left on the plates!

These times of the Covid-19 pandemic presented a challenge for everyone worldwide. A call to care for us and love ourselves in a different, more personal and committed way. For Paul Council, my husband, and myself it represented a time of expressing our loving, sharing our physical space, our productive and leisure time in a new and sometimes challenging way.

My love for cooking and his love for photography brought us together in this project that we happily share with you. We invite you to join us and enjoy these recipes and what they represent for us, while taking care of ourselves at home in these times of pandemic. It is a journey experienced through the kitchen that connected us with our lived experiences, places visited and even those we want to visit in the future. Thank you very much for accepting this invitation!

The time will come to share and embrace our loved ones again, to visit the places we want to and connect with nature, culture and flavors that we are going to enjoy there. In the meantime, we will continue to care and love each other, hoping all of you will do the same.

Receive our gratitude and a big hug of support, love and seasoning in these times of quarantine.

THANKS

Thank you, God for being present in my life and guide me with so much Love.

Paul Council, thank you for joining me, taking care of me and loving me. I love you

Thank you, Gabriela Mata for being an essential part of this project.
Thank you very much for everything!

To my friends Kenny Aliaga and Jacques Giraud, without your advice and support
I wouldn´t have the focus needed to finish and make this a reality.
Big hug to both of you!

Thanks to everyone who in one way or another have been part of my life and
growth on this planet. Thank you for the shared teachings, laughter, sadness,
challenges, achievements and learnings. I carry them in my heart today and always.

To all the scientific community and health care workers in the world,
who with so much effort, perseverance and loving will take care of us
and guide us until we overcome this pandemic. My gratitude goes out to you,
all of your family and loved ones. Thank you very much!

DEDICATION

To Magdalena and Bartolome Mata, my parents,
who always have been the best example of love in my life.

To Pirula (Valentina Silva) and Amanda Sanchez,
who spoiled me and taught me so much love in the kitchen.

CONTENTS

SOUPS & CREAMS

SIDES & SALADS

ENTRÉES

Chicken Breast on Spicy Honey, Mustard & Sesame Sauce	46
Shredded Chicken Salad Reina Pepiada Style	48
Lamb Chops with Mint Sauce	50
Pork Stew Mata Family Style	52
Eggplant Boats Stuffed with Ground Beef & Eggs	54
Pork Chops in an Orange, Rum & Basil Sauce	56
Steak Kebabs	58
Spicy Ground Beef for Tacos	60
Stuffed Meatballs with Tomato Sauce	62
Stuffed Bell Peppers with Ground Beef	64
Fillet Mignon with a Mushroom & Horseradish Sauce	66
Pan Seared Octopus with Lemon Potatoes	68
Stuffed Tomatoes with Tuna Salad	70

Salmon Fillet Cooked in a Shrimp, Peppers & Capers Velouté	72
Fried Calamari with Marinara Sauce	74
Multicolor Sea Bass Ceviche	76
Fried Halibut Sticks with Tartar Sauce	78
Shrimp in a Spicy Coconut Milk Sauce	80
Wild Tuna with a Ginger and Sage Chutney	82
Wild Cod in a Leeks, Capers & Herbs Sauce	84
Seafood Salad Salpicón Style	86
Salmon Tartare	88
Fish Tacos	90

DESSERTS

Amanda's Pineapple Quesillo	94
Tres Leches	96

SOUPS
& CREAMS

"Soup is to a meal
as the overture is to an opera"

Jean Anthelme Brillant-Savarin - 1826

BROCOLLI & CHEDDAR CREAM

This is one of the classic American delicious soups to enjoy, it is warm, welcoming and flavorful. A perfect way to celebrate being on the land of the free and the home of the brave.

4 PORTIONS   **15**min PREP TIME   **25**min COOKING TIME

Ingredients

1 cup of diced red onions (yellow or white onions work as substitute)

10 oz of broccoli florets

1/2 lb of shredded cheddar cheese

2 cups of chicken stock (vegetable works as substitute)

3 cups of water

1/2 cup of heavy cream

3 Tbsp. of corn starch

2 Tbsp. of butter

Salt

Ground black pepper (ground white pepper works as substitute)

Preparation

1 In a deep pot over medium heat, put to melt the butter with a splash of extra virgin olive oil (other vegetable oil work as substitute). After the butter is melted, add the onions and 1/2 tsp. of salt and let it cook for 2 minutes, until transparent. Add the chicken stock, water and broccoli florets. Bring it to a boil, cover the pot and cook for 7 minutes. Turn off the heat.

2 Blend the cream using a regular blender or a hand blender. Make sure that no chunks of broccoli or onions are left inside the cream.

3 Turn on the heat to a medium level and add the shredded cheddar cheese, stir with a wooden spoon so the cheese integrates evenly into the cream, add 1/2 tsp. of salt and 1/2 tsp. of ground black pepper.

4 In a small container add the corn starch and 4 Tbsp. of water at room temperature. Mix it vigorously until it completely dissolves in the water. Add this mixture to the cream and stir until it thickens evenly. Add the heavy cream and keep stirring until the cream gets to boil, turn the heat off. Taste the cream and add more salt and pepper if needed. Enjoy!

CORN, SHRIMP & ANDOUILLE SAUSAGE CHOWDER

4 PORTIONS   25 min PREP TIME   25 min COOKING TIME

This recipe, that mixes land and sea products in a delicious way, is a symbol of how combining cultures, races, backgrounds and histories creates amazing and unique results…
For Paul and for me, this has been our experience as a couple, and the best is yet to come!

Preparation

1 In a deep pot over medium heat, put the butter to melt and add a splash of extra virgin olive oil (any other vegetable oil work as substitute) add the diced onions and 1/2 tsp. of salt, stir fry for 2 minutes with a wooden spoon, until transparent. Add the andouille sausage and the minced garlic, stir fry for 3 minutes, until it gets a little golden.

2 Add the shrimp stock and the water, diced potatoes, corn kernels and spicy paprika, 1/2 tsp. of salt and 1/2 tsp. of ground white pepper. Bring the soup to a boil, cover the pot and let it cook for 10 minutes. Cut the peeled shrimp in 2 or 3 parts (leave them whole if you prefer), add them to the chowder while is still boiling. Cook for 2.5 minutes and then turn the heat to a very low level.

3 In a small container add the corn starch and 4 Tbsp. of water at room temperature. Mix it vigorously until it completely dissolves in the water. Add this mixture to the chowder and stir until it thickens evenly. Add the heavy cream and the parsley, increase the heat to a medium level, bring the soup to a boil while stirring, turn the heat off. Taste the chowder and add salt and pepper if needed.

4 Garnish it by slicing the radishes (use a mandoline for better results, using it with extra precautions). Separate the leaves and also slice them finely. Place the sliced bulbs on top of the chowder once it has been poured on the soup bowls, add a bunch of the sliced radish greens on top. Enjoy!!!

Ingredients

1/2 lb of peeled raw shrimp

1/2 lb of corn kernels (raw or frozen)

1/2 lb of diced andouille sausage

1/2 cup of diced red onions (yellow or white onions work as substitute)

1/2 cup of diced red potatoes (white or yellow potatoes work as substitute)

2 Tbsp. of butter

2 minced garlic cloves

1/2 cup of heavy cream

2 cups of water

2 cups of shrimp stock (fish stock, vegetable stock or chicken stock work as substitute)

1/2 tsp. of spicy paprika (sweet paprika works as substitute)

3 Tbsp. of corn starch

1 Tbsp. of minced fresh parsley (dry parsley works as substitute)

Salt

Ground white pepper (ground black pepper works as substitute)

Garnish

2 Radishes with the greens

MUSHROOM CREAM

You can use this recipe to create different vegetable creams, just substitute the mushrooms with asparagus, celery, leeks, or any other veggie you can think of. The idea is to use our creativity to expand our loving and playing around with flavors, colors and textures…

4 PORTIONS   **20**min PREP TIME   **25**min COOKING TIME

Ingredients

11 oz of diced mushrooms

1/2 cup of diced red onions (yellow or white onions work as substitute)

2 minced garlic cloves

2 cups of chicken stock (vegetable stock works as substitute)

3 cups of water

3 Tbsp. of butter

1/2 cup of heavy cream

3 Tbsp. of corn starch

2 Tbsp. of minced fresh parsley (dry parsley works as substitute)

1/4 tsp. of grounded nutmeg

Salt

Ground white pepper (ground black pepper works as substitute)

Preparation

1 In a deep pot over medium heat put the butter to melt with a splash of olive oil (vegetable oil works as substitute). Add the diced red onions and 1/2 tsp. of salt, cook it for 2 minutes and then add the minced garlic cloves. Add the diced mushrooms and cook it for 4 minutes, stirring from time to time with a wooden spoon, don't let it brown too much.

2 Add the chicken stock and the water, 1 tsp. of salt and 1/2 tsp. of ground pepper, increase the heat to a medium-high level and bring it to a boil. Cover the pot, reduce the heat to a low level and let it cook for 8 minutes.

3 In a small container add the corn starch and 4 Tbsp. of water at room temperature. Mix it vigorously until it completely dissolves in the water. Add this mixture to the cream and stir until it thickens evenly. Add the heavy cream, nutmeg and minced parsley, increase the heat to a medium level and keep stirring until the cream gets to boil, turn the heat off. Taste the cream and add salt and pepper if needed. Enjoy!

BLACK BEANS, RED BELL PEPPER & TORTILLA SOUP

4	15 min	25 min
PORTIONS	PREP TIME	COOKING TIME

When we published the pictures of this soup on social media, it was a big hit! The explosion of flavors is as colorful as it is to our eyes…

Preparation

1 In a deep pot over medium heat, put the extra virgin olive oil and let it heat for 1 minute. Add the onions and 1/2 tsp. of salt, let it cook for 2 minutes, until transparent. Add the red bell peppers and cook for 2 minutes. Open the can of black beans and add all of its content, no need to drain it. Stir with a wooden spoon and let it cook for 3 minutes.

2 Add the chicken stock and the water, red pepper paste, and stir everything until it dissolves. Cover the pot with a lid and bring everything to a boil. Reduce the temperature to a low level and let it cook for 10 minutes, stirring occasionally. Add the hot sauce, 1 Tbsp. of minced cilantro, 1/2 tsp. of black ground pepper and 1/2 tsp. of salt. Taste the soup and add salt and pepper if needed.

3 To serve, add to a soup bowl 1/4 cup of raw shredded cabbage and a handful of tortilla chips crumbs (you can make them by hand). Add the soup quantity that you desire, finish the presentation with more tortilla chips (crumbs or whole as desired) and 1/4 tsp. of minced cilantro. Enjoy!

Ingredients

1 cup of diced red bell pepper

1 cup of diced red onions (yellow or white onions works as substitute)

1 can of 15 oz of black beans (kidney beans work as substitute)

2 Tbsp. of red pepper paste (tomato paste works as substitute)

2 cups of chicken stock (vegetable stock works as substitute)

2 cups of water

2 Tbsp. of extra virgin olive oil (any other vegetable oil works as substitute)

2 Tbsp. of minced fresh cilantro (dry cilantro works as substitute)

1 cup of shredded raw cabbage

Tortilla chips

2 tsp. of hot sauce chili based (optional)

Salt

Ground black pepper (ground white pepper works as substitute)

SPINACH CREAM

This is my favorite soup since when I was a kid, I imitated my father by adding two or three spoons of cooked white rice to it, that made me feel so grown up!

4	20min	25min
PORTIONS	PREP TIME	COOKING TIME

Ingredients

5 oz of washed spinach leaves

1 cup of diced red onions (yellow or white onions work as substitute)

1 lb of red potatoes (yellow or white potatoes work as substitute)

2 cups of chicken stock (vegetable stock works as substitute)

3 cups of water

1/2 cup of heavy cream

2 Tbsp. of butter

Salt

Ground black pepper (ground white pepper works as substitute)

Preparation

1 In a deep pot over medium heat, put to melt the butter with a splash of extra virgin olive oil (other vegetable oil works as substitute). After the butter is melted, add the onions and 1/2 tsp. of salt and let it cook for 2 minutes, until transparent.

2 Clean the potatoes and cut them in quarts (the skin of the potatoes adds an earthy flavor to the cream, but you can peel them if preferred) add them to the pot, the chicken stock and the water, 1/2 tsp. of salt and 1/2 tsp. of ground pepper. Cover the pot and bring it to a boil, let it cook for 10 minutes, until the potatoes are soft. Turn off the heat and add the spinach leaves. Push then down with the wooden spoon so they get submerged in the stock. Cover the pot and let it sit for 2 minutes.

3 Blend the cream using a regular blender or a hand blender. Make sure that no chunks of potatoes or spinach are left inside the cream.

4 Turn on the heat to a medium level and add the heavy cream, if the consistency is too thick add 1/4 cup of water. Bring everything to a boil while stirring. Turn off the heat, cover the pot with a lid and let it sit for 2 minutes. Taste the cream and add salt and pepper if needed. Serve and Enjoy!

ONION SOUP

This soup lifts our spirit and brings warmth and coziness
to our hearts and souls, it is ideal for cold winter days…

4 PORTIONS   **20**min PREP TIME   **40**min COOKING TIME

Preparation

1 In a deep pot over medium heat, put the butter to melt with a splash of extra virgin olive oil (other vegetable oil works as substitute). Once the butter is melted, add the sliced onions and 1/2 tsp. of salt. Cover the pot with a lid and let it cook for 25 minutes stirring every 3 minutes with a wooden spoon. The idea is to caramelize the onion slices without burning them.

2 Add the beef stock and water, minced garlic, fresh parsley, 1/2 tsp. of ground black pepper and bring everything to a boil. Cover the pot with a lid and cook for 5 minutes.

3 In a small container add the corn starch and 4 Tbsp. of water at room temperature. Mix it vigorously until it completely dissolves in the water. Add this mixture to the soup and stir until it thickens evenly. Turn down the heat to a low level. Taste the soup and add more salt and pepper if needed.

4 Cut the edges of the bread slices and then in a diagonal cut to create two triangles (if desired, you can use a cookie cutter to create different shapes), cover them with a thick layer of shredded parmesan cheese. Place them in a baking sheet, toast the slices in the oven at 350° F for 5 minutes, making sure the toast edges brown and the parmesan cheese melts on top the toasts, if needed toast for a longer time. Serve the soup while is still hot, and put two triangle toasts on top of it. Enjoy!!!!

Ingredients

1 lb of white onions finely sliced vertically from top to bottom -émincé style- (yellow or red onions work as substitute)

4 Tbsp. of butter

2 minced garlic cloves

4 cups of beef stock (chicken stock works as substitute)

2 cups of water

1 Tbsp. of minced fresh parsley (dry parsley works as substitute)

3 Tbsp. of corn starch

4 slices of bread

Shredded parmesan cheese

Salt

Ground black pepper (ground white pepper works as substitute)

TOMATO CREAM

This is one of Paul's favorite soups. He loves it with cubes of mozzarella cheese and sliced fresh basil. He has given me feedback over the years to make it better and better every time. The same way we have made each other better through our loving.

4 PORTIONS **20**min PREP TIME **25**min COOKING TIME

Ingredients

1.5 lb of ripe tomatoes (Beefsteak or Roma kind)

6 oz of tomato paste

1 cup of red onion grossly chopped (yellow or white onions work as substitute)

2 cups of chicken stock (vegetable stock works as substitute)

2 cups of water

3 Tbsp. of corn starch

1/2 cup of heavy cream

2 Tbsp. of extra virgin olive oil

1 tsp. of paprika

1/2 Tbsp. of oregano

8 leaves of fresh basil

Salt

Ground black pepper (ground white pepper works as substitute)

Preparation

1 With a sharp knife, make 2 perpendicular small cuts at the bottom end of each tomato. Put them in a pot over high heat, fill it up with enough water until they are covered and bring it to a boil, cook for 1 minute. Take the tomatoes out and submerge them for 3 minutes in a bowl with enough cold water and Ice.
Take the tomatoes out and peel them starting with the edges created at the cuts made at the bottom. Cut them in quarts and seed them. Reserve them in a bowl.

2 In a deep pot over medium heat, put the extra virgin olive oil and let it heat for 1 minute. Add the onions and 1/2 tsp. of salt, stir fry with a wooden spoon for 2 minutes, until transparent. Add the peeled and seeded tomatoes, chicken stock and oregano, bring it to a boil. Cover the pot and let it cook for 10 minutes. Turn off the heat of the stove.

3 Blend the cream using a regular blender or a hand blender. Make sure that no chunks of tomatoes or onions are left inside the cream.

4 Turn on the heat to a medium level and add the water, paprika, tomato paste, 1/2 tsp. of salt and 1/2 tsp. of ground black pepper, stir to incorporate all the ingredients. Bring the cream to a boil and reduce the heat to a medium-low level.

5 In a small container add the corn starch and 4 Tbsp. of water at room temperature. Mix it vigorously until it completely dissolves in the water. Add this mixture to the soup and stir until it thickens evenly. Add the heavy cream and keep stirring until the cream gets to a boil, turn the heat off. Taste the cream and add salt and pepper if needed. Just before serving it, cut the basil leaves in thin slices and distribute them evenly on each soup bowl. Enjoy!

LEEK & CORN CREAM

The crispiness of the leaks with the sweetness of the corn creates a fresh combination, like butter and jelly on toast!

4 PORTIONS	15 min PREP TIME	25 min COOKING TIME

Preparation

1 In a deep pot over medium heat, put the butter to melt and add a splash of extra virgin olive oil (other vegetable oil works as substitute). After the butter has melted add the sliced leeks, 1/2 tsp. of salt and 1/2 tsp. of ground black pepper, stir fry with a wooden spoon for 2 minutes. Add the chicken stock, water and corn kernels. Cover the pot and bring it to a boil, reduce the heat to a low level and cook it for 10 minutes. Turn off the heat.

2 Blend the cream using a regular blender or a hand blender. Make sure that no chunks of leeks and corn kernels are left inside the cream.

3 In a small container add the corn starch and 4 Tbsp. of water at room temperature. Mix it vigorously until it completely dissolves in the water. Add this mixture to the cream and stir until it thickens evenly. Add the heavy cream, turn on the heat to a medium level and keep stirring until it gets to boil, turn the heat off. Cover the pot and let it sit for 2 minutes. Taste the cream and add salt and pepper if needed. Enjoy!

Ingredients

1/2 lb of sliced washed leeks

1/2 lb of corn kernels (raw or frozen)

2 Tbsp. of butter

1/2 cup of heavy cream

3 cups of water

2 cups of chicken stock (vegetable stock works as substitute)

3 Tbsp. of corn starch

Salt

Ground black pepper (ground white pepper works as substitute)

SHRIMP CREAM THAI STYLE

Thailand is on our bucket List for our travels, and the entire South East Asia region. We love to travel and expand our horizons, taste new flavors and live new experiences… here is our advice, travel as much as you can! In the mid time, especially during this pandemic, travel with us in your kitchen!

4 PORTIONS   **15** min PREP TIME   **25** min COOKING TIME

Ingredients

1 lb of peeled raw shrimp

1/2 cup of diced red onions (white or yellow onions work as substitute)

1/2 lb of diced mushrooms

2 minced garlic cloves

1 can (13.5 oz) of coconut milk

3 cups of shrimp stock (chicken, fish or vegetable stock work as substitute)

2 fresh lemongrass bulbs cut in halves (1 Tbsp. of dry lemongrass works as substitute)

2 Tbsp. of hot sauce (optional)

2 Tbsp. of coconut oil (extra virgin olive oil works as substitute)

3 Tbsp. of corn starch

Salt

Ground white pepper (ground black pepper works as substitute)

Preparation

1 In a deep pot over medium heat, put the coconut oil and let it heat for 1 minute, add the diced onions and 1/2 tsp. of salt, stir fry with a wooden spoon for 2 minutes, until transparent. Add the diced mushrooms and the garlic cloves, cover the pot with a lid and cook for 3 minutes stirring occasionally.

2 Add the shrimp stock, coconut milk, lemon grass, 1/2 tsp. of salt and 1/2 tsp. of ground white pepper, bring everything to a boil, reduce the temperature to a medium-low level, cover the pot and cook for 5 minutes. Add the hot sauce (optional) and the raw shrimp, increase the heat to a medium level, wait until the soup boils, cover it and cook for 2.5 minutes.

3 In a small container add the corn starch and 4 Tbsps. of water at room temperature. Mix vigorously until it completely dissolves in the water. Add this mixture to the cream and stir until it thickens evenly, keep stirring until the cream gets to a boil, turn the heat off. Taste the cream and add salt and pepper if needed. Enjoy!

SIDES
& SALADS

"Friends are the bacon bits
in the salad bowl of life"

Anonymous

CAULIFLOWER, LEEKS & CELERY CASSEROLE

Due to the lockdown, I had the opportunity to grow veggies on our terrace, leeks and celery among them. Hence the creation of this recipe, it was creating something literally from scratch!

4 PORTIONS **20**min PREP TIME **90**min COOKING TIME

Ingredients

10 oz of cauliflower florets. (Fresh or frozen)

10 oz of leek trunks

10 oz of celery sticks

4 Tbsp. of all-purpose flour

4 Tbsp. of butter

2 cups of cold whole milk

2 cups of grated parmesan cheese

1/4 tsp. of ground nutmeg

Salt

Ground white pepper (ground black pepper works as substitute)

Preparation

1 In a sauce pan over medium heat put the butter to melt and add a splash of extra virgin olive oil (any other vegetable oil works as substitute), once it has melted add the all-purpose flour and stir with a wooden spoon, so it would create a thick paste. Add 4 Tbsp. of cold milk and stir vigorously until it's integrated, then add 4 more Tbsp. of cold milk and stir until is integrated, repeat the same procedure with 6 Tbsp. of milk and then slowly increment the volume of liquid until adding all of it. The idea is to create a white sauce without crumbs. Add the nutmeg, 1/2 tsp. of salt and 1/2 tsp. of ground white pepper. Keep stirring the sauce until it starts to boil. Turn off the heat and reserve on the side.

2 Cut the celery sticks in halves and then in squares, put them in a small bowl. Cut the Leek trunks in halves and then slice them, put them in another small bowl.

3 Butter all the inner surfaces of a 10"x8" tempered glass (Pyrex) container. Place the leek slices, then the celery squares and then the cauliflower florets in a way that they are layered and distributed evenly. Sprinkle on top 1/4 tsp. of salt and 1/4 tsp. of ground white pepper. Add on top of the vegetables a layer of the thick white sauce, covering them evenly. Sprinkle on top of it the grated parmesan cheese covering all the surface of the casserole.

4 Cover the casserole with aluminum foil and bake in the oven at 350° F for 1 hour. Remove the aluminum foil cover, and let it bake uncovered for 10 minutes, until there is a golden crust on top of the casserole. Take it out and let it rest uncovered 5 minutes before serving. Enjoy!

CAPRESE SALAD

This is a perfect example that sometimes less is more! The key is using fresh ingredients, ripe tomatoes and you will be happy to share this salad as a side, or an appetizer… or maybe a midnight snack?

4 PORTIONS   **15**min PREP TIME   **0**min COOKING TIME

Preparation

1 Cut the tomatoes in halves, and make thick wedges from them, sprinkle on top 1/2 tsp. of salt and 1/2 tsp. of ground black pepper.

2 Cut the fresh mozzarella in halves and make thick slices of them. Cut the basil leaves in quarts

3 Divide the tomato wedges, slices of mozzarella cheese and basil leaves quarts in 4 parts. Assemble each salad by layering tomato, mozzarella cheese and basil leaves.

4 Sprinkle each salad with 2 Tbsp. of extra virgin olive oil and 1/2 tsp. of balsamic vinegar. Add more salt and pepper if needed. Enjoy!

Ingredients

2 lb of Beefsteak tomatoes. (Campari or Roma tomatoes work as substitute)

8 oz of fresh mozzarella cheese

16 leaves of fresh basil

8 Tbsp. of extra virgin olive oil

2 tsp. of balsamic vinegar (red wine vinegar works as substitute)

Salt

Ground black pepper (ground white pepper works as substitute)

GUACAMOLE

The best Guacamole in New York City,
according to Paul. The time I lived in Chile changed
my life for the better, and I am so grateful for that.
I used to dislike avocados (big time), until I moved there…
What a change! And how wonderful avocados are!

4 PORTIONS   **25**min PREP TIME   **0**min COOKING TIME

Ingredients

3 ripe hass avocado of 1/2 lb each

1/2 cup of minced red onions (yellow or white onions work as substitute)

1/3 cup of diced spring onions

1/3 cup of diced bell peppers (red or yellow preferable)

2 minced garlic cloves

2 limes (lemon works as substitute)

2 Tbsp. of minced fresh cilantro (dry cilantro works as substitute)

4 Tbsp. of extra virgin olive oil

1/2 Tbsp. of hot sauce (optional)

Salt

Ground white pepper (ground black pepper works as substitute)

Preparation

1 In a bowl place the onions, bell peppers, spring onions, garlic, cilantro and mix all together.

2 Pit the avocados by making a cut with a chef knife lengthwise all around it. Twist each half of the avocado in an opposite direction with your hands and separate them. Take out the pit of the half that still have it by sticking the knife edge lengthwise and twist it, the pit should stick to the knife. Using a metal spoon separate the flesh out of the skin of each half of the avocado. Put them inside the bowl, squeeze the limes on top of them, add the extra virgin olive oil, 1/2 tsp. of salt, 1/2 tsp. of ground white pepper and hot sauce.

3 Using a fork, smash the avocado flesh against the bottom and sides of the bowl, making sure there are not big chunks of flesh left. Mix everything together until all gets incorporated and create the texture you desire. If you like it creamier, add a little bit of olive oil, if you like it thinner, add a little bit of water. Taste it and add more salt, pepper and hot sauce if needed. Enjoy!!!

MIXED SALAD

Fresh, healthy, colorful, delicious…

4 PORTIONS **20**min PREP TIME **0**min COOKING TIME

Preparation

1 Slice the lettuce and put them in a big bowl, add the cucumbers, tomatoes, radishes, bell peppers and hearts of palm.

2 Pit the avocado by making a cut with a chef knife lengthwise all around it. Twist each half of the avocado in an opposite direction with your hands and separate them. Take out the pit of the half that still have it by sticking the knife edge lengthwise and twist it, the pit should stick to the knife. Separate the flesh out of the skin of each half of the avocado with a metal spoon. Slice it and add them to the salad.

3 Add the paprika, sugar, extra virgin olive oil, squeeze the lime on top, add 1/2 tsp. of ground black pepper and 1/2 tsp. of salt.

4 Using 2 spoons, toss all the ingredients within the bowl, making sure everything gets well mixed. Taste the salad and add more salt and pepper if needed. Enjoy!

Ingredients

5 oz of romaine lettuce washed (any other kind of lettuce work as substitute)

1 cup of thick sliced cucumbers cut in halves

2 cups of Campari tomato wedges cut in halves (Roma kind works as substitute)

1/2 cup of sliced radishes cut in halves

1/2 cup of sliced seeded red bell peppers (any color bell pepper work as substitute)

1/2 cup of sliced heart of palms

1 ripe hass avocado

1/2 tsp. of paprika

6 Tsp. of extra virgin olive oil

1 lime (lemon works as substitute)

1/2 tsp. of sugar

Salt

Ground black pepper (ground white pepper work as substitute)

MUSHROOM RISOTTO

Pizza, pasta and risotto! These for me, and for many, are the three most popular and known foods from the lovely Italy. You can make this delicious dish with other vegetables or proteins, like asparagus or squash, squid, chicken or shrimp, your imagination and creativity will lead your way to make the perfect risotto.

4 PORTIONS **25**min PREP TIME **30**min COOKING TIME

Ingredients

2 cups of arborio rice

12 oz of diced white mushrooms (baby bella mushrooms work as substitute)

1 cup of finely diced red onions (white or yellow onions work as substitutes)

3 minced garlic cloves

3 Tbsp. of minced fresh parsley (dry parsley works as substitute)

6 Tbsp. of butter

3 cups of chicken stock (vegetable stock works as substitute)

3 cups of water

1/2 cup of grated parmesan cheese

1/4 cup of extra virgin olive oil

Salt

Ground black pepper (ground white pepper works as substitute)

Preparation

1 In a deep pot over medium heat, put 4 Tbsp. of butter to melt and add a splash of extra virgin olive oil (other vegetable oil works as substitute), add the diced onions and 1/2 tsp. of salt, stir fry with a wooden spoon for 2 minutes, until transparent. Add the diced mushrooms, minced garlic and parsley, stir fry for 10 minutes, until the mushrooms get golden-brown.

2 While the mushrooms are cooking, put in a small sauce pan over medium heat. the chicken broth and cups of water and bring them to a boil. After the mushrooms are cooked, add the arborio rice, 1/2 tsp. of salt and 1/2 tsp. of ground black pepper, stir vigorously and mix everything. Add 1 cup of the hot liquid mix and stir 2 or 3 times to incorporate the liquid to the solid mix. Turn down the heat to a low level and let it cook until the level of liquid reduces below the level of rice and mushrooms.

3 Add 1/2 cup of the liquid mix and stir again to incorporate the liquid to the solid mix, let it cook until the level of liquid reduces below the level of rice and mushrooms. Repeat this process until you have used all the broth and water mix.

4 Add the grated parmesan cheese, extra virgin olive oil and 2 Tbsp. of butter. Stir everything until all the ingredients are incorporated, taste the risotto and add salt and pepper if needed. Cover the pot and let it sit for 2 minutes. Serve and Enjoy!

GREEK SALAD

Traveling to Greece is definitely on our bucket list, we love Greek food, we will certainly love everything else there!

4 PORTIONS   **20**min PREP TIME   **0**min COOKING TIME

Preparation

1 Slice the lettuce and put them in a big bowl, add the cucumbers, tomatoes, olives, onions and feta cheese.

2 Add the sumac, extra virgin olive oil, balsamic vinegar, 1/2 tsp. of ground pepper and 1/2 tsp. of salt.

3 Using 2 spoons, toss all the ingredients within the bowl, making sure everything gets well mixed. Taste the salad and add more salt or pepper if needed. Enjoy!

Ingredients

4 oz of romaine lettuce, washed (any other kind of lettuce works as substitute)

2 cups of thick sliced cucumbers cut in halves

2 cups of Campari tomato wedges cut in halves (Roma kind works as substitute)

1/2 cup of sliced Kalamata olives

1/4 cup of sliced red onions (yellow or white onions work as substitute)

1 cup of feta cheese cubes of 1/2"

1/2 tsp. of sumac

6 Tbsp. of extra virgin olive oil

3 Tbsp. of balsamic vinegar (red wine vinegar works as substitute)

Salt

Ground black pepper (ground white pepper works as substitute)

ENTRÉES

"This is my invariable advice to people:
learn how to cook, try new recipes,
learn from your mistakes,
be fearless and above all have fun!"

Julia Child - 2004

CHICKEN BREAST ON A SPICY HONEY, MUSTARD & SESAME SAUCE

4
PORTIONS

25min
PREP TIME

35min
COOKING TIME

Ingredients

2 lb of chicken breasts

1 cup of red onions grossly chopped (yellow or white onions work as substitute)

1/2 cup of broccoli florets

1 cup of red bell peppers grossly chopped (green or yellow bell peppers work as substitute)

1/2 cup of celery sticks grossly chopped

3 minced garlic cloves

6 Tbsp. of honey

3 Tbsp. of Dijon mustard

1/4 cup of water

1 Tbsp. of sesame seeds

2 tsp. of hot sauce (optional)

1/2 tsp. of sesame oil

3 Tbsp. of extra virgin olive oil (any vegetable oil works as substitute)

Salt

Ground black pepper (ground white pepper works as substitute)

This is a sweet, sour and spicy sauce that pairs great with the chicken's neutral flavor. Try it with the Cauliflower, Leeks & Celery Casserole in this book and you will enjoy and share a feast!

Preparation

1 Cut the chicken breasts in halves and then each half in 4 parts. Salt and pepper all the pieces and reserve in a bowl.

2 In a large deep pan over high heat, add the extra virgin olive oil and let it heat for 1 minute. Add 4 pieces of the chicken breast with enough space between them so their juices don't mix up, sear them until golden-brown, flip the pieces and sear them again until the other side is also golden-brown. Take the pieces out and reserve them in another bowl. Repeat this process for all the chicken pieces.

3 Reduce the temperature to a medium level, add the onions, bell peppers, celery, garlic, 1/2 tsp. of salt, 1/2 tsp. of ground black pepper and the sesame oil. Stir fry for 2 minutes with a wooden spoon. Add the golden-brown pieces of chicken, water, honey, Dijon mustard, hot sauce and sesame seeds. Bring everything to a boil, reduce the heat to a low level, cover the pan with a lid and let it simmer for 12 minutes. Stir everything to make sure the consistency of the sauce is even and all the flavors are integrated. Taste the sauce and add more salt, pepper or hot sauce if needed. Turn off the heat and let it sit for 2 minutes before serving. Enjoy it!

SHREDDED CHICKEN SALAD REINA PEPIADA STYLE

This is "La Reina" (The Queen) of stuffing for arepas in my home country, Venezuela. I pray every day for our freedom, justice and recovery of democracy…

4 PORTIONS	2 hrs 30 min PREP TIME	10 min COOKING TIME

Preparation

1 In a medium pot over medium heat, place the chicken breasts and cover them with water, add 1 tsp. of salt, bring it to a boil, cover with a lid and cook for 10 minutes. With a slotted spoon, place the chicken breasts in a small container with a lid and put them in fridge for at least 2 hours. Reserve the stock left in the pot to use in other recipes.

2 Shred the cold chicken in a big bowl, add the onions and the cilantro on top. Pit the avocados by making a cut with a chef knife lengthwise all around it. Twist each half of the avocado in an opposite direction with your hands and separate them. Take out the pit of the half that still have it by sticking the knife edge lengthwise and twist it, the pit should stick to the knife. Using a metal spoon separate the flesh out of the skin of each half of the avocados, put them on top of the rest of the ingredients in the bowl.

3 Squeeze the limes on top of the avocados, add the mayonnaise and hot sauce, 1 tsp. of salt and 1/2 tsp. of ground black pepper. With a fork smash the avocados' flesh and incorporate all the ingredients into a paste making sure to create an even profile through the salad. Taste it and add more salt, pepper and hot sauce if needed. Enjoy!

Ingredients

1.2 lb of boneless chicken breasts

2 ripe hass avocados of 1/2 lb each

1/2 cup of minced red onions (white or yellow onions work as substitute)

4 Tbsp. of minced fresh cilantro (dry cilantro works as substitute)

2 limes (lemons work as substitute)

4 Tbsp. of mayonnaise

2 Tbsp. of hot sauce (optional)

Salt

Ground black pepper (white ground pepper works as substitute)

LAMB CHOPS WITH MINT SAUCE

Paul and I have a lot of common ground in terms of favorite foods. Lamb is one of them. This recipe brings together the sweetness and freshness of the mint to the earthy and charred flavor of the lamb chops, a perfect combination enjoyed by generations!

4 PORTIONS   **45** min PREP TIME   **25** min COOKING TIME

Ingredients

2.5 lb of lamb chops

1/2 cup of minced red onions (yellow or white onions work as substitute)

4 Tbsp. of butter

1 Tbsp. of sugar

Salt

Ground black pepper (ground white pepper work as substitute)

For the Mint Sauce

1 cup of finely sliced fresh mint. (2/3 cup of dry mint works as substitute)

1/2 cup of white wine vinegar (sherry vinegar or apple cider vinegar works as substitute)

1/4 cup of sugar

1/8 tsp. of salt

Preparation

1 In a small sauce pan over medium heat, place the white wine vinegar and sugar, stir until it dissolves completely. Bring it to a boil and let it cook for 2 minutes, so it reduces the volume and creates a syrup. Turn off the heat, add the mint leaves and salt, stir to incorporate all the ingredients. Reserve the sauce on the side, letting it cool down for at least 20 minutes.

2 Salt and pepper the lamb chops just before starting the preparation of the recipe. In a large pan over high heat, add 2 Tbsp. of butter and let it melt, add 1 Tbsp. of sugar and stir with a wooden spoon until it dissolves in the butter, heat it for 90 seconds and place up to 4 lamb chops with enough space that their juices will not mix, sear for 2 minutes so their bottom side browns and then flip them on the other side and sear them for another 2 minutes, until they brown as well. Take them out of the pan and put them in a separate bowl. Repeat this process until all the lamb chops have been seared brown on both sides.

3 Reduce the heat to a medium-low level and add the other 2 Tbsp. of butter, onions, 1/2 tsp. of salt and 1/2 tsp. of ground black pepper; stir fry with a wooden spoon for 2 minutes until transparent. Add the lamb chops back to the pan and place them together. Add the mint sauce, bring everything to a boil, cover the pan with a lid and let it cook for 3 minutes, flip the chops to the other side, cover the pan again and let it cook for another 3 minutes. Turn off the heat.

4 Check the doneness of the lamb chops by pressing gently with your index finger on top of the meat, if it is too soft means that the chop is medium or medium rare, the harder it feels, the chops are more done. I personally like them medium to medium-well. You can increase or reduce the cooking time to achieve the level of doneness you desire. Cover the pan and let it sit for 2 minutes until serve. Taste the sauce and add more salt and pepper if needed. Add sliced fresh mint leaves just before serving. Enjoy!

PORK STEW MATA FAMILY STYLE

4
PORTIONS

1 hr
PREP TIME

1 hr 15 min
COOKING TIME

This stew is inspired on the Hallacas stuffing we enjoy for Christmas and the Holidays. This abbreviated version, carries the savory, sweet and sour flavors that are so distinctive of the Venezuelan food.
It is a connection to family, traditions and loving…

Preparation

1 Cut the pork loin in dices of 1'', salt and pepper them and reserve in a bowl on the side. Cut the green olives and the cocktail onions in halves and reserve them in a small bowl.

2 In a large pot over medium heat, put the extra virgin olive oil and let it heat for 1 minute. Add the onions, carrots, celery, bell peppers, 1/2 tsp. of salt and 1/2 tsp. of black ground pepper. Stir with a wooden spoon, cover with a lid and cook for 2 minutes.

3 Add the pork dices to the pot, capers, stuffed green olives, cocktail onions, raisins, yellow mustard, Worcestershire sauce, Moscato wine, minced fresh oregano, hot sauce and sugar. Mix everything, lower the heat to a low level, cover the pot and cook for 1 hour, mixing it every 15 minutes. Turn off the heat and let it sit for 3 minutes. Taste the stew and add salt and pepper if needed. Enjoy!

Ingredients

2.5 lb of pork loin

2 cups of diced red onions (yellow or white onions work as substitute)

1 cup of diced celery

1 cup of diced carrots

1 cup of diced red bell peppers (any other color of bell peppers works as substitute)

1/3 cup of capers

1 cup of green olives stuffed with red peppers (pitted green olives works as substitute)

1/2 cup of cocktail onions

3/4 cup of raisins

1/2 cup of yellow mustard (Dijon mustard works as substitute)

3 Tbsp. of Worcestershire sauce

3 Tbsp. of minced fresh oregano (dry oregano works as substitute)

3 Tbsp. of hot sauce (optional)

3 Tbsp. of sugar

3 Tbsp. of extra virgin olive oil (other vegetable oil works as substitute)

1/2 cup of Moscato wine

Salt

Ground black pepper (ground white pepper works as substitute)

EGGPLANT BOATS STUFFED WITH GROUND BEEF & EGGS

This recipe has elements of Greek flavors, but with a bit of imagination it is also a twist on the Chilean "empanada de pino" stuffing. For me this is how cultures and flavors fuse into new ideas and experiences. I hope you enjoy this as much as we do!

4 PORTIONS **30**min PREP TIME **90**min COOKING TIME

Ingredients

1.3 lb of ground beef

1 cup of diced red onions (yellow or white onions work as substitute)

1 cup of diced red bell peppers (any color of bell peppers works as substitute)

1/2 cup of diced celery

1 tsp. of paprika

1/2 tsp. of ground cumin

4 minced garlic cloves

2 eggplants of 1.2 lb each

2 hard-boiled eggs peeled

24 pitted Kalamata olives

8 oz of feta cheese cut in small dices (crumbled feta cheese works as substitute)

Extra virgin olive oil

Salt

Ground black pepper (ground white pepper works as substitute)

Preparation

1 Cut the eggplants in halves. Scoop out the flesh of each half, using a metal spoon, leaving a 1/2" layer of flesh from the skin. The idea is to create 4 boats where the stuffing will be placed. Brush or spray a thin layer of extra virgin olive oil covering the interior surfaces of the eggplant boats. Cut the eggplant flesh previously scooped out in small pieces and reserve on the side.

2 In a large pan over medium-high temperature, add 3 Tbsp. of extra virgin olive oil and heat for 1 minute. Put the diced onions and add 1/2 tsp. of salt, stir fry for 2 minutes with a wooden spoon, until transparent. Add the diced bell peppers, celery, minced garlic and the eggplant flesh previously cut in small pieces. Stir fry for 5 more minutes.

3 Add the ground beef and spread it evenly using all the surface of the pan. Add 1 tsp. of salt, 1 tsp. of ground black pepper, paprika and ground cumin. Lower the heat to a medium level and let it cook for 15 minutes, stirring every 2 minutes. Turn off the heat, taste it and add more salt and pepper if needed.

4 Cut the hard-boiled eggs lengthwise in halves, cut each half lengthwise in 2, the result is 8 quarts with egg white and yolk included.

5 Divide the ground beef, eggplant and veggies stuffing in 4 even parts. Spread half of a stuffing part in the bottom of one of the eggplant boats, creating an even surface. Starting from one end of the boat, place 2 Kalamata olives side to side, 1 hard-boiled egg quart, 2 Kalamata olives, another hard-boiled egg quart and finish with 2 Kalamata olives. The idea is to place these elements perpendicular to the length of the eggplant boat. Put the rest of the stuffing part on top of the olives and hard-boiled eggs leaving them partially uncovered in some areas. Repeat this step with the other 3 eggplant boats.

6 Cover a baking sheet (15" x 10") with aluminum foil, sprinkle a little of extra virgin olive oil on top, place the eggplant boats one next to the other. Bake them at 350° F for 30 minutes. Take the baking sheet out of the oven very carefully, cover each eggplant boat with 2 oz. of feta cheese dices and bake them for 20 minutes more. Take everything out of the oven and let it sit for 3 minutes before serving. Enjoy!

PORK CHOPS IN AN ORANGE, RUM & BASIL SAUCE

Orange, rum and basil sounds like a great drink!!
If you want to make it and pair it with this creation, go for it!
The idea is to have fun in the kitchen, the dining room
and all around the house.

4 PORTIONS **15** min PREP TIME **50** min COOKING TIME

Preparation

1 Salt and pepper the pork chops, reserve on the side.

2 In a large fry pan over high heat, put the butter to melt and add a splash of extra virgin olive oil (other vegetable oil works as substitute), let it heat for 2 minutes, until it browns a little. Place the pork chops, in batches of 2 pieces at a time, to sear for 3 minutes until they brown, flip them and sear the other side for another 3 minutes, until they brown as well. Take them out and put them in a plate, complete this process for all the pork chops.

3 Reduce the heat to medium–low level, add the red onions and 1/2 tsp. of salt, stir fry with a wooden spoon for 2 minutes, until transparent. Place the pork chops back into the pan, squeeze the oranges on top and add the squeezed orange wedges to the pan. (Add the orange juice if you are using it instead of the oranges). Add the rum, minced garlic cloves, paprika, basil, hot sauce, 1/2 tsp. of salt and 1/2 tsp. of ground black pepper. Bring it to a boil, cover the pan with a lid and cook for 15 minutes. Flip the pork chops, cover the pan again and cook them for 15 minutes more. Turn off the heat, let it sit for 2 minutes. Discard the squeezed wedges, taste the sauce and add more salt and pepper if needed. Chop a few fresh basil leaves and sprinkle them on top of the chops before serving. Enjoy!

Ingredients

2 lb of boneless pork chops, 1/2'' thick (2.5 lb if you use chops with bones)

2 oranges (1 cup of orange juice works as substitute)

1/2 cup of rum

1/2 cup of finely diced red onions (yellow or white onions work as substitute)

2 minced garlic cloves

1/2 cup of chopped fresh basil (2 Tbsp. of dry basil work as substitute)

1 Tbsp. of hot sauce (optional)

4 Tbsp. of butter

1 tsp. of spicy paprika (sweet paprika works as substitute)

Salt

Ground black pepper (ground white pepper works as substitute)

STEAK KEBABS

My dear friend Diana Barake taught me how to make these amazing kebabs. They totally transport me back to Lebanon and the amazing flavors of Beirut. We pray that this beautiful city and its people will recover to be again the Paris of the Middle East.

4 PORTIONS

2hrs **30**min PREP TIME

25min COOKING TIME

Ingredients

4 sirloin medallions 12 oz each

2 large size (or 3 medium) red onions (yellow or white works as substitute)

2 large size (or 3 medium) red bell peppers (yellow or orange works as substitute)

8 cherry tomatoes.

4 Tbsp. of red pepper paste (tomato paste works as substitute)

1 lime (lemon works as substitute)

1/3 cup of white vinegar

1 Tbsp. of coriander

2 Tbsp. of minced fresh parsley (dry parsley works as substitute)

Salt

Ground white pepper (ground black pepper works as substitute)

8 bamboo kebab skewers of 12" (metal skewers work as substitute)

Preparation

1 In a large bowl mix the pepper paste, white vinegar, coriander, parsley, 2 tsp. of salt and 4 tsp. of ground white pepper. Squeeze the lime juice on top and mix until all the ingredients are well integrated.

2 Cut the sirloin medallions in 8 even pieces. To do this cut each medallion in half (1/2), then each part in half (1/4) and then each part in half (1/8). The final result should be 32 even parts. Marinate the pieces in the mix spices paste, make sure all of them are well rubbed with the paste. Cover the bowl with saran wrap or aluminum foil and let marinate for at least 2 hours, preferably inside the fridge.

3 Put the 8 bamboo skewers in a container with water, in a way that they are fully in contact with the water, this will help to prevent them to catch fire while cooking the kebabs.

4 Cut the red onions in quarts. Separate the layers of the onion by cutting the bottom end of the quart that holds it together. Reserve the largest pieces. The idea is to have 64 layers of onions. Cut the bell peppers in quarts and seed them. Cut each quart in 8 even pieces. The idea is to have 64 pieces of bell peppers.

5 Assemble the kebabs by holding a skewer with one hand, start threading 2 pieces of bell pepper, then 2 layers of onions, 1 piece of steak and then repeat the process 3 more times. Each kebab should have 4 pieces of beef, 8 layers of onions and 8 pieces of peppers. Create an evenly distributed kebab by putting all the pieces tightly together.

Finish each kebab with a cherry tomato, the tip of the skewer should come out at least 1/2" from it, this will make easier to manage it while cooking. Start assembling the kebab 1" from the bottom of the skewer and keep all the pieces tightly together.

6 Cook the kebabs on the grill at a medium-high temperature, rotate the kebabs over the heat every 3 or 4 minutes to avoid burning them (the veggies and the tips of the steak will create a burnt layer, but don't overdo this). They should be ready in about 15 to 20 minutes, but this also depends on the grill temperature and how done you desire the beef to be. Once they are cooked, take them out of the grill and let them sit in a tray 2 minutes before serving. Enjoy!

SPICY GROUND BEEF FOR TACOS

Pair it with the Guacamole recipe in this book, with some sour cream, fresh cilantro leaves, over corn or flour tortillas, and you get a delicious beef taco meal!

4 PORTIONS   **15**min PREP TIME   **35**min COOKING TIME

Preparation

1 In a large pan over medium-high heat, put the extra virgin olive oil and let it heat for 1 minute. Add the diced onions and 1/2 tsp. of salt, stir fry for 2 minutes with a wooden spoon, until transparent. Add the diced bell peppers and the minced garlic cloves. Cook for 2 more minutes, stirring occasionally.

2 Add the ground beef and spread it evenly using all the surface of the pan. Add 1 tsp. of salt, 1 tsp. of ground black pepper, the oregano, cilantro, raisins and Worcestershire sauce. Reduce the temperature to a low level, cover the pan and cook for 5 minutes.

3 Using a wooden spoon, break the ground beef into smaller pieces, add the hot sauce and stir everything to incorporate the flavors and create an even profile. Cover again and cook for 20 minutes stirring every 5 minutes. Turn off the heat, let it sit for 2 minutes. Taste the ground beef and add more salt and pepper if needed. Enjoy!

Ingredients

1.3 lb of ground beef

2 cups of diced red onions. (yellow or white onions work as substitute)

1 cup of diced red bell peppers (any color works as substitute)

1/2 cup of raisins (optional)

3 Tbsp. of Worcestershire sauce

3 minced garlic cloves

2 Tbsp. of hot sauce (optional)

2 Tbsp. of minced fresh oregano (dry oregano works as substitute)

1 Tbsp. of minced fresh cilantro (dry cilantro works as substitute)

2 Tbsp. of extra virgin olive oil

Salt

Ground black pepper (ground white pepper works as substitute)

Ingredients

1 1/2 lb of ground beef

1 cup of finely diced red onions (yellow or white onions work as substitute)

6 minced garlic cloves

2 eggs

2 Tbsp. of Worcestershire sauce

1/2 cup of bread crumbs

2 Tbsp. of minced fresh oregano (dry oregano works as substitute)

2 Tbsp. of minced fresh parsley (dry parsley works as substitute)

2 Tbsp. of minced fresh basil (dry basil works as substitute)

1 Tbsp. of crushed peppers flakes (optional)

2 sticks of mozzarella string cheese

16 pepperoni slices

1 can of 28 oz of crushed tomatoes. (canned tomato puree work as substitute)

2 Tbsp. of tomato paste

1/2 cup of water

2 Tbsp. of extra virgin olive oil

Salt

Ground black pepper (ground white pepper works as substitute)

STUFFED MEATBALLS WITH TOMATO SAUCE

Perfect to enjoy over spaghetti or white rice.
Pair them with the Caprese Salad recipe in this book and presto!
An amazing Italian dinner!

Preparation

1 In a large bowl put the ground beef, add 1/2 cup of the finely diced onions, 4 minced garlic cloves, eggs, Worcestershire sauce, bread crumbs, 1 Tbsp. of oregano, 1 Tbsp. of parsley, 1 Tbsp. of basil, crushed peppers flakes, 1 1/2 tsp. of salt and 1 tsp. of ground black pepper. Using your hands, mix everything together until all the ingredients are well incorporated.

2 Cut each mozzarella cheese string sticks in 8 equal parts and reserve on the side. Cut the peperoni slices in quarts, also reserve them on the side. Weight the ground beef using a scale, and divide the mix in 16 equal parts. Wet your hands in water and create a small ball with one of the ground beef portions, press the ball to create a disk evenly thick 2" in diameter. Place 2 pepperoni slice quarts in the middle of the disk, put on top 1 dice of mozzarella cheese and then 2 pepperoni slice quarts. Wrap these pieces with the edges of the ground beef disk and create a meatball making sure to seal the cheese inside the ground beef.
Put it in a plate or in a board avoiding to stack them on top of each other. Repeat this process until all the 16 stuffed meatballs are completed.

3 In a large pot over medium heat, put the extra virgin olive oil to heat for 30 seconds, add the rest of the diced onions and 1/2 tsp. of salt, stir fry with a wooden spoon for 2 minutes, until transparent.
Add 2 minced garlic cloves, canned crushed tomatoes, tomato paste, 1 Tbsp. of oregano, 1 Tbsp. of parsley, 1 Tbsp. of basil, 1 tsp. of salt, 1/2 tsp. of ground black pepper and 1/2 cup of water. Stir occasionally and bring everything to a boil.

4 Place the meatballs inside the large pot, stacking them the least possible, so they are covered with the tomato sauce, and bring it back to a boil. Cover with a lid, reduce the heat to a medium-low level and cook for 12 minutes.

Flip the meatballs carefully, cover the pot again and cook for 12 minutes more.

Turn off the heat and let it sit for 2 minutes. Taste the sauce and add more salt and pepper if needed. Enjoy!

STUFFED BELL PEPPERS WITH GROUND BEEF

4 PORTIONS 40min PREP TIME 1hr 40min COOKING TIME

This is one of my favorite recipes to make on a weekend. I can relax and enjoy doing other things while it is cooking in the oven, the aroma of the bell peppers while cooking spreads all over our place… and excellent prelude for our dinner.

Preparation

1 Cut the top of each bell pepper 3/4'' from the top. With a small and sharp knife cut out the seeds and internal white veins, discard any seeds attached to the top of the bell peppers. Reserve them on the side.

2 In a medium bowl place the ground beef, red onions, cherry tomatoes, black olives, garlic, red pepper flakes, oregano, parsley, paprika, hot sauce and Worcestershire sauce. Add 1 tsp. of salt and 1/2 tsp. of ground black pepper. Mix everything making sure that all the ingredients are evenly incorporated.

3 Stuff each bell pepper bottom, press gently the stuffing so all the cavities are filled up. Put enough stuffing so it will over flow about 1/2'' over the top border. Cover the bell peppers with its correspondent top previously cut and seeded.

4 Grease the bottom of a 12''x10'' tempered glass (Pyrex) container with extra virgin olive oil. Put the stuffed bell peppers inside the container. Cover with aluminum foil and place it in a metal baking tray. Place everything in the oven at 350° F for 90 minutes. Uncover the glass tempered container and bake for 10 minutes more, so the top of the bell peppers brown. Take the tray out of the oven and let is sit for 3 minutes. Serve the stuffed bell peppers on top of rice and bathe them with the sauce that sits at the bottom of the container. Enjoy!

Ingredients

4 orange bell peppers large (red, yellow or green bell peppers work as substitute)

1 lb of ground beef

1 cup of diced red onions (white or yellow onions work as substitute)

3/4 cup of diced cherry tomatoes (Roma or Campari tomatoes work as substitute)

1/2 cup of sliced black olives

4 minced garlic cloves

1 Tbsp. of red pepper flakes (crushed red pepper)

2 Tbsp. of minced fresh oregano (dry oregano works as substitute)

2 Tbsp. of minced fresh parsley (dry parsley works as substitute)

1 tsp. of spicy paprika (sweet paprika works as substitute)

2 Tbsp. of Worcestershire sauce

2 Tbsp. of hot sauce (optional)

2 Tbsp. of extra virgin olive oil

Salt

Ground black pepper (ground white pepper works as substitute)

FILET MIGNON WITH A MUSHROOM & HORSERADISH SAUCE

This delicious dish worth all the Zumba classes and bicycle rides to Coney Island to get rid of the calories that it brings to the table (and to our bodies), trust us… it is amazingly flavorful!!!!

4
PORTIONS

25min
PREP TIME

35min
COOKING TIME

Ingredients

2 Filet Mignon
(beef tenderloin stakes) of 1 lb each

4 strips of bacon
(8 if they are not wide enough)

4 wooden toothpicks
(8 if using 8 bacon strips)

6 oz of sliced mushrooms

3 Tbsp. of prepared horseradish

6 Tbsp. of butter

1/2 cup of heavy cream

2 Tbsp. of fresh parsley
(dry parsley works as substitute)

3 minced garlic cloves

Salt

Ground black pepper (ground white
pepper works as substitute)

Preparation

1 Cut the Filet Mignon in halves, wrap each half with a strip of bacon and secure the end of it with a wooden toothpick, make sure the wrap is tight. (if the strips are not wide enough to cover the steak from the top to bottom, use 2, side to side, and use 2 toothpicks to secure each strip). Salt and pepper the top and bottom of the steak (which should not be wrapped in bacon). Reserve on the side.

2 In a large fry pan over high heat, put 4 Tbsp. of butter to melt and add a splash of extra virgin olive oil (other vegetable oil works as substitute) and let it heat for 2 minutes. Place the bottom side of the Filet Mignon steaks on the fry pan and sear them for 2 minutes. Flip them and put the top side facing the pan, sear for another 2 minutes. Turn the Filets on their side (the wrapping bacon should be facing the bottom of the fry pan), and sear for 2 minutes, flip them and put the other side facing the bottom of the pan and sear for 2 minutes, repeat this process 2 more times until all the sides wrapped with bacon have been seared. Reduce the temperature to a medium-low level and take the fillets out of the pan and put them in a plate.

3 Add in the pan the sliced mushrooms, horseradish, parsley, garlic, 2 spoons of butter, 1/2 tsp. of salt and 1/2 tsp. of ground black pepper. Stir fry for 2 minutes using a wooden spoon. Return the Filet Mignon to the pan, cover it and cook everything for 5 minutes. Add 1/2 cup of heavy cream, stir with a wooden spoon to incorporate the cream, flip the steaks, cover the pan and cook for 3 minutes. Turn off the heat and let it sit for 2 minutes. Taste the sauce and add more salt and pepper if needed. Enjoy!

PAN SEARED OCTOPUS WITH CAPERS & LEMON POTATOES

4 PORTIONS **20**min PREP TIME **1**hr **20**min COOKING TIME

Ingredients

2 lb of raw octopus tentacles

4 Tbsp. of capers

4 Tbsp. of extra virgin olive oil

2 lemons (limes work as substitute)

3 minced garlic cloves

Salt

Ground black pepper (ground white pepper works as substitute)

For the lemon potatoes

1 1/2 lb of white potatoes (yellow or red potatoes work as substitute)

5 Tbsp. of butter

2 lemons (limes work as substitute)

1 Tbsp. of minced fresh oregano (dry oregano works as substitute)

Salt

Ground black pepper. (ground white pepper works as substitute)

We love octopus, so we invite you to share this loving with us. Cooking it is easier than you may think and the results are very tasty!

Preparation

1 In a medium pot over medium heat, put 4 cups of water and bring it to a boil. Add the octopus and 1 tsp. of salt, bring back to a boil, cover it and cook for 35 minutes. Take out the octopus and submerge it in a bowl with enough water with ice. Once the octopus is cold, drain the water and reserve the octopus tentacles on the side. Reserve the stock where the octopus has been cooked so you can use it in other recipes.

2 In a large pan over high heat, put 2 Tbsp. of extra virgin olive oil and heat it for 30 seconds. Put the octopus tentacles inside the pan in batches of 3, with enough space between them so their juices won't mix, cook each side of the tentacles for 4 minutes so they get golden-brown. Take them out of the pan and reserve on a plate. Once all the octopus' pieces have gone through this process, turn down the heat to a medium low level and put back all the cooked tentacles inside the pan. Squeeze the lemon on top of everything and add the squeezed wedges to the pan, add the capers, minced garlic, 1/2 tsp. of salt, 1/2 tsp. of ground black pepper and 2 Tbsp. of extra virgin olive oil. Cover the pan with a lid and cook for 15 minutes, stirring every 3 minutes. Turn off the heat and let it sit for 2 minutes. Discard the lemon wedges, taste the sauce and add salt and pepper if needed.

Lemon Potatoes

1 Wash thoroughly the potatoes and cut them in quarts.

2 In a large pan over medium-high heat, put the butter to melt and add a splash of olive oil (other vegetable oil works as substitute). Once the butter is melted, place the potatoes with one of the inner faces down to the pan, so all the skins are facing up, cook them for 2 minutes. Put the other inner side of the potato quarts to face the pan and cook them for 2 minutes. Check to see if the potatoes have brown to a desired level and when this is achieved, reduce the heat to a medium-low level and turn the potatoes around, so all of their skin side are in direct contact with the pan.

3 Squeeze the lemon on top of everything and add the squeezed wages to the pan. Add the oregano, 1/2 tsp. of salt and 1/2 tsp. of ground black pepper. Cover it with a lid and cook for 6 minutes, until the potatoes are soft but maintain their form. If the skins are detaching from the potatoes, that means they are starting to overcook, so we want to avoid that. Discard the lemon wages, taste the sauce and add more salt and pepper if needed. Serve them with the octopus and enjoy!

STUFFED TOMATOES WITH TUNA SALAD

This dish is for me the perfect summer dinner, even better if it is near a beach. It is almost like being in Playa Zaragoza, Margarita Island, one more time… a piece of heaven on earth. Where is yours?

4 PORTIONS **40**min PREP TIME **0**min COOKING TIME

Preparation

1 Cut each tomato about 1/4'' from the top. Using a sharp short knife and a teaspoon take out the seeds and inner flesh of the tomatoes, reserve them for other recipes.

2 In a medium bowl, place the tuna from the drained cans, onions, celery, bell peppers, cilantro, mayonnaise, hot sauce, squeeze the lemons on top, add 1/2 tsp. of salt and 1/2 tsp. of ground black pepper. Mix all the ingredients together until create a homogeneous paste. Taste it and add more salt and pepper if needed.

3 Stuff each tomato with the tuna salad and partially cover them with the top, put enough salad so it will come out about 1/2'' over the edge of the tomatoes, that way when the top is partially placed over the paste, it creates a space so the tuna salad can be seen. Serve them on top of rice or green salad.

Enjoy!

Ingredients

8 Beefsteak tomatoes of 1/2 lb each

2 cans of tuna, drained, of 7 oz net each

1 cup of diced red onions (white or yellow onions work as substitute)

1/2 cup of diced celery

1 cup of diced yellow bell pepper (any other color works as a substitute)

8 Tbsp. of mayonnaise

2 Tbsp. of minced fresh cilantro (dry cilantro works as substitute)

2 tsp. of hot sauce (optional)

2 limes (lemons work as substitute)

Salt

Ground black pepper (ground white pepper works as substitute)

SALMON FILLET COOKED IN A SHRIMP, PEPPERS & CAPERS VELOUTÉ

4 PORTIONS **20**min PREP TIME **45**min COOKING TIME

My mom used to cook for us red snapper or grouper fillets with a similar sauce, and we loved it! For me this was an opportunity to follow the proverb "when life gives you lemon, make lemonade" During the pandemic, life gave me salmon… so I created this.

Ingredients

4 wild caught salmon fillets with skin, approx. 8 oz each (farmed salmon works as a substitute)

5 Tbsp. of butter

2 Tbsp. of capers

1 lime (lemon works as a substitute)

2 Tbsp. of all-purpose flour

1 cup of finely chopped red onions (white or yellow onions work as substitute)

1/2 cup of finely chopped red bell peppers (orange or yellow bell pepper work as substitute)

1/2 cup of finely chopped celery

1 cup of grossly chopped raw peeled shrimp

1 cup of cold shrimp stock (fish stock works as substitute)

2 cups of cold whole milk

2 minced garlic cloves

1/4 tsp. of ground nutmeg

Salt

Ground white pepper (ground black pepper works as substitute)

Preparation

1 Check the Salmon fillets and take out any bones if necessary, using tweezers. Salt and pepper them and reserve on the side while preparing the velouté sauce.

2 In a sauce pan over medium heat, add 3 Tbsp. of butter and a splash of extra virgin olive oil (other vegetable oil works as substitute). After all the butter is melted, add the onions and 1/2 tsp. of salt, stir fry for 2 minutes with a wooden spoon, until transparent. Add the red bell peppers, celery and garlic, stir fry for 2 more minutes. Add the all-purpose flour and stir constantly everything to incorporate it with the fat of the butter and all the other ingredients, keep stirring for 1 minute more.

3 Reduce the heat to a low level, add 1/4 cup of cold shrimp stock and stir everything until incorporates completely. Repeat this step 3 mores times, until all the shrimp stock is incorporated. Add 1 cup of cold milk and keep stirring and incorporating, at this point the sauce should have a thick and even consistency, add the remaining cup of cold milk and stir until the sauce is homogeneous and have a glossy texture.
Increase the heat to a medium level, add the grossly chopped raw shrimp and the capers, nutmeg, 1/2 tsp. of white ground pepper and 1/2 tsp. of salt. Cook for 3 minutes, stirring occasionally. Turn off the heat and reserve on the side.

4 In a large pan over medium heat, put 2 Tbsp. of butter to melt with a splash of olive oil (other vegetable oil works as substitute). Heat it for 2 minutes until it browns a little. Put the 4 salmon fillets with the skin side facing the pan. Let them cook for 1 minute. Squeeze the lime on top of the fillets and put the squeezed wedges inside the pan. Incorporate the shrimp and veggies velouté on top of them, cover the pan, reduce the heat to a medium-low level and cook for 5 minutes. Turn off the heat and let it sit, for 2 minutes. Discard the squeezed wedges. Taste the sauce and add salt and pepper if needed. Serve the fillets with sauce on top of them, making sure that pieces of shrimp and veggies sit on top of the salmon. Enjoy!

FRIED CALAMARI WITH MARINARA SAUCE

Is this an appetizer or main course to share?
We particularly love the crunchiness of this recipe,
seems that there is always room for one more piece!

Ingredients

1 lb of fully cleaned calamari tubes and tentacles (if preferred, only tubes)

2 limes (lemons work as substitute)

1 cup of whole milk (buttermilk works as substitute)

2 cups of all-purpose flour

2 tsp. of paprika

2 Tbsp. of minced fresh oregano (dry oregano works as substitute)

2 Tbsp. of minced fresh parsley (dry parsley works as substitute)

Corn oil (Canola or other vegetable oil work as a substitute, except olive oil

Salt

Ground white pepper (ground black pepper works as substitute)

For the marinara sauce

1/4 cup of finely diced red onions (white or yellow onions work as substitute)

2 minced garlic cloves

1 can of 14.5 oz of crushed tomatoes (canned tomatoes puree work as substitute)

1 Tbsp. of tomato paste

1/2 cup of water

1 tsp. of sugar

1 Tbsp. of minced fresh oregano (dry oregano works as substitute)

1 Tbsp. of fresh minced basil (dry basil works as substitute)

2 Tbsp. of extra virgin olive oil

Salt

Ground black pepper (ground white pepper works as substitute)

Preparation

1 Cut the squid tubes in rings of 1" thick. The tentacles heads can be left wholes or cut in halves if desired. Put them in a glass or plastic bowl and squeeze the limes on top of them. Mix everything with a wooden spoon, cover it with saran wrap and put it in the fridge for at least 30 minutes. (An airtight container also works for this process)

2 In 2 separate bowls put in each one of them 1 cup of all-purpose flour, 1 tsp. of paprika, 1 tsp. of salt, 1/2 tsp. of ground white pepper, 1 Tbsp. of oregano and 1 Tsp. of parsley. Mix everything in each bowl, to create an even flavor profile on each mix. In a third bowl, put the cup of whole milk.

3 Using tongs or your fingertips, put 3 or 4 pieces of calamari in the first bowl of the flour and spices mix, shake them so they get all covered with the dry mix. Take them from the first bowl and submerge then in the milk in the second bowl for 5 seconds, making sure that they get all covered with milk. Using a fork take them out of the milk and place them in the third bowl, with the flour and spices mix that was not used before, shake it to cover them with it. Place them in a plate or a board covered with paper towels. Complete this process for all the pieces of squid, and use as many plates or boards covered with paper towels, so you don't pile the pieces on top of each other.

4 In a deep fry pan over medium heat, put the corn oil (or other vegetable oil different than olive oil) enough to fill the pan around 3/4 of its capacity. Let it heat for 4 minutes. Put to fry 8 to 10 pieces (depending of the size of the deep fry pan it could be smaller or larger batches)

The idea is that the pieces float in the oil without overcrowding it. Let the pieces fry for about 2 to 3 minutes, flipping them around from time to time, until golden. Take them out with a slotted spoon and place them in a big bowl covered with paper towel, sprinkle a little bit of salt on top.

Marinara Sauce

1 In a small saucepan over medium heat, put the extra virgin olive oil, add the onions and 1/2 tsp. of salt, stir fry with a wooden spoon for 2 minutes, until transparent. Add the garlic, canned crushed tomatoes, tomato paste, water, sugar, oregano, basil, 1/2 tsp. of salt and 1/2 tsp. of ground black pepper. Mix it until the tomato paste dissolves in the sauce.

2 Bring the sauce to a boil, cover the saucepan with a lid, lower the temperature to a medium-low level and cook for 5 minutes. Turn off the heat, and let it sit covered for 2 minutes. Taste the sauce and add more salt and pepper if needed. Serve the sauce with the calamari and enjoy!!!

MULTICOLOR SEA BASS CEVICHE

This creation is an homage to my Latin and Andean roots. Even though Venezuela is known as a Caribbean country, with beautiful beaches and tropical climate, the Andes mountains end (or begin?) in our country and connects us with Colombia, Ecuador, Perú, Bolivia, Argentina and Chile. Hope you can join us in this colorful and delicious journey!

4	2hrs 40min	0min
PORTIONS	PREP TIME	COOKING TIME

Preparation

1 In a small bowl put the onions and add 1 tsp. of salt and mix it, cover with a plastic saran wrap, put it in the fridge and let it sit for at least 2 hours. (An airtight container also works for this process).

2 Cut the sea bass fillets in dices of about 1.5", place them inside a medium size bowl (plastic or glass container, avoid using metal) add the tri-color bell peppers slices, 1/2 tsp. of salt, 1/2 tsp. of ground white pepper, hot sauce and the minced garlic, mix everything together. Squeeze the limes on top of all the ingredients, the fish cubes should be submerged in the lime juice. Cover the bowl with saran wrap, put it in the fridge and let it sit for at least 2 hours. (You can use an airtight container instead)

3 Just before serving, take out the onions from the container with a fork and add them to the bowl where the ceviche has been marinating, the slices should be transparent and flexible since they have released all the water inside of them. Discard the water left in the container where the onions were. Add the cilantro and sliced radish, mix all together making sure to create an even flavor and color profile in the ceviche. Taste it and add salt, pepper and hot sauce if needed. Enjoy!

Ingredients

1.5 lb of sea bass fillets

1 cup of red onions cut finely sliced vertically from top to bottom -émincé style- (yellow or white onions work as substitute)

1/3 cup of finely sliced red bell peppers about 2" long.

1/3 cup of finely sliced green bell peppers about 2" long.

1/3 cup of finely sliced yellow bell peppers about 2" long.

1/4 cup of finely sliced radish cut in half

2 minced garlic cloves.

8 Limes (lemons work as substitute)

1 Tbsp. of hot sauce (optional)

2 Tbsp. of minced fresh cilantro (dry cilantro works as substitute)

Salt

Ground white pepper (ground black pepper works as substitute)

FRIED HALIBUT STICKS WITH TARTAR SAUCE

Ingredients

1 1/2 lb of skinned halibut fillets (cod, grouper, sea bass or snapper work as substitute)

2 eggs

2 Tbsp. of all-purpose flour

1/4 cup of whole milk

1/2 tsp. of paprika

2 cups of plain bread crumbs

1 Tbsp. of minced fresh oregano (dry oregano works as substitute)

1 Tbsp. of minced fresh parsley (dry parsley works as substitute)

Corn oil (any vegetable oil works as substitute, except olive oil)

Salt

Ground black pepper (ground white pepper works as substitute)

For the tartar sauce

1 cup of mayonnaise

1 cup of finely diced dill pickle

1/2 cup of finely diced red onions (white or yellow onions work as substitute)

3 Tbsp. of sour cream

1/2 tsp. of black ground pepper (white ground pepper works as substitute)

2 Tbsp. of minced fresh dill (dry dill works as substitute)

1 Tbsp. of minced fresh parsley (dry parsley works as substitute)

2 Tbsp. of capers

1 lime (lemon works as substitute)

During the pandemic Paul got for us harvested in-season halibut delivered from Alaska, as a way for us to connect with our trip over there 3 years ago. I created this recipe and he expressed that he got at home the best halibut sticks of the lower 48… He was elated and I was happy for creating this special moment for the two of us.

Preparation

1 Cut the halibut fillets in 2"x1/2"x1/2" pieces (or the shape that you desire, according to the length and thickness of the fillets you have). Salt and pepper the pieces and reserve on the side.

2 In a bowl scramble the eggs, add the all-purpose flour, whole milk, 1/2 tsp. of salt, 1/4 tsp. of ground black pepper and mix everything together. In a separate bowl, place the bread crumbs, paprika, parsley, oregano and mix everything to create an even flavor profile.

3 In batches of 2 or 3 pieces, submerge them in the egg, flour and milk batter for 5 seconds, making sure it covers all the surfaces of the fish pieces, take them out using tongs and place them in the second bowl with the seasoned bread crumbs. Shake it until the pieces are covered with the mix, place them in a plate or a board covered with paper towel, avoid stack them on top of each other. Complete this process for all the fish pieces and use as many plates or boards covered with paper towels, so you don't pile the pieces on top of each other.

4 In a deep fry pan over medium heat, put the corn oil (or other vegetable oil different than olive oil) enough to fill the pan around 3/4 of its capacity. Let it heat for 4 minutes. Put to fry 3 to 4 pieces (depending of the size of the deep fry pan it could be smaller or larger batches). The idea is to fry the pieces for 2 minutes without touching each other. Flip them with a slotted spoon and fry for 2 minutes more or until they reach the golden-brown shade desired. Take them out of the oil and place them in a big bowl covered with paper towel.

Tartar Sauce

❙ In a medium bowl place the mayonnaise, dill pickle, red onions, sour cream, dill, parsley, capers and black ground pepper. Squeeze the lime on top of everything. Mix all the ingredients well and serve in a small container with the fried fish. Enjoy!!!

SHRIMP IN A SPICY COCONUT MILK SAUCE

4 PORTIONS   **15**min PREP TIME   **20**min COOKING TIME

This recipe works well if you substitute the protein with fish, chicken, lamb or even tofu. Just modify the cooking time on step 3 accordingly to cook properly the chosen protein substitute. I personally like to make this with shrimp because it elevates the flavor profile and color with the sauce, but maybe if you are allergic, vegetarian or don't like seafood, making a substitution would be a nice way to enjoy this delicious dish.

Ingredients

2.5 lb of peeled raw shrimp

1 cup of red onions cut finely sliced vertically from top to bottom -émincé style- (yellow or white onions work as substitute)

1 cup of sliced celery

1 can of coconut milk (13.5 oz)

1 Tbsp. of red pepper paste (tomato paste works as substitute)

2 Tbsp. of fresh sliced basil (dry basil work as substitute)

1/2 tsp. of sesame oil

2 Tbsp. of coconut oil (extra virgin olive oil works as substitute)

3 Tbsp. of hot sauce (optional)

Salt

Ground black pepper (ground white pepper works as substitute)

Preparation

1 In a large pan over medium heat, put the coconut oil to heat for 1 minute, add the sliced onions and 1/2 tsp. of salt, stir fry with a wooden spoon for 2 minutes, until transparent. Add the sesame oil and the sliced celery and stir fry for 1 minute.

2 Add the coconut milk, red pepper paste, hot sauce, 1/2 tsp. of salt, 1/2 tsp. of ground black pepper and bring everything to a boil, stirring occasionally to make sure all the ingredients integrate evenly.

3 Add the shrimp to the sauce, cover the pan and let it cook for 4 minutes. Stir the shrimp in the sauce and make sure to flip them, especially those on the top. Cover again and let it cook for 3 minutes. Sprinkle on top the sliced fresh basil, stir everything to integrate them to the sauce, turn off the heat, cover the pan and let it sit for 2 minutes. Taste the sauce and add salt and pepper if needed. Enjoy!

WILD TUNA WITH GINGER & SAGE CHUTNEY

4 PORTIONS **20**min PREP TIME **25**min COOKING TIME

Ingredients

4 wild tuna steaks, 1/2 lb each

1 cup of finely diced red onions (yellow or white onions work as substitute)

1/2 cup of finely diced yellow bell peppers (any other color bell pepper works as substitute)

4 minced garlic cloves

1/2 cup of finely sliced fresh sage leaves (dry sage works as substitute)

1/2 cup of minced fresh cilantro (dry cilantro works as substitute)

3 limes (lemons work as substitute)

6 Tbsp. of butter

3 Tbsp. of ginger paste

1 Tbsp. of sugar

Salt

Ground white pepper (ground black pepper works as substitute)

This is the recipe that started it all. I was really proud of this creation and also grateful for the positive response it got on social media. Then the idea of putting together these recipes and share them with you came along and almost inevitably, one after the other showed up as a way to connect us with our loving and with you in these quarantine times.

Preparation

1 In a large pan over medium heat, put the butter to melt and add a splash of extra virgin olive oil (other vegetable oil works as substitute), let it heat for 1 minute. Add the diced onions, and 1/2 tsp. of salt, stir fry with a wooden spoon for 2 minutes, until transparent. Add the diced bell peppers, sliced sage leaves, 1/2 tsp. of ground white pepper and the minced garlic cloves. Cook all together stirring for 2 more minutes.

2 Salt and pepper the tuna steaks. Increase the heat to a medium-high level and move the base of the chutney to the sides of the pan to create a clear surface. Put the tuna stakes in the pan and sear them for 2 minutes. Flip the steaks and sear the other side for 2 minutes.

3 Reduce de heat to a low level, squeeze the limes on top of the tuna steaks, add the squeezed wedges inside the pan, add the minced cilantro, ginger paste, sugar and 1/2 tsp. of salt. Cover with a lid and cook for 10 minutes. At this stage they should be cooked to a medium-well level, you can increase or decrease the cooking time depending on how cooked you like them and also how thick the steaks are.

4 Turn off the heat and let it rest for 2 minutes before serve. Discard the lemon wedges, take the tuna steaks out and plate them accordingly, mix the chutney with a wooden spoon, taste it and add salt and pepper if needed. Serve it on top of the tuna stakes. Enjoy!

WILD COD IN A LEEKS, CAPERS & HERBS SAUCE

Cod is for me one of the best fish to cook and enjoy on a dish, a great combination of texture and flavor. It has its own distinctive personality!

4 PORTIONS **20**min PREP TIME **20**min COOKING TIME

Preparation

1 Cut the wild cod fillets in 8 pieces of approximately 1/4 lb. each. Salt and pepper them and reserve in a plate or a bowl.

2 In a large pan over medium heat, put the butter to melt with a splash of extra virgin olive oil (other vegetable oil works as substitute) let it heat for 90 seconds. Add the leeks, greens onions, sage, 1/2 tsp. of salt and 1/2 tsp. of ground white pepper. Stir fry with a wooden spoon for 2 minutes.

3 Move the leeks, greens onions and sage to the edges of the base of the pan to create a clean surface in the middle. Place the wildcCod pieces in the pan, add the thyme, dill and capers, squeeze the lime on top of everything and add the squeezed wedges to the pan. Cover with a lid, reduce the heat to a medium-low level and let it cook for 12 minutes. Turn off the heat and let it sit for 2 minutes. Discard the squeezed wedges and taste the sauce, add more salt and pepper if needed. Enjoy!

Ingredients

2 lb of wild cod fillets

2 cups of sliced leeks cut in halves

1/2 cup of sliced green onions

2 Tbsp. of capers

1/2 cup of sliced fresh sage (dry sage works as substitute)

2 Tbsp. of minced fresh thyme (dry thyme works as substitute)

2 Tbsp. of minced fresh dill (dry dill works as substitute)

8 Tbsp. of butter

2 limes (lemons work as substitute)

Salt

Ground white pepper (ground black pepper works as substitute)

SEAFOOD SALAD SALPICÓN STYLE

My mom loved making this dish, from getting fresh products at the fishermen's market to cooking everything and sharing it with our family and friends. This recipe connects me with my roots in Margarita Island, of great times in paradise here on Earth…

Ingredients

1/2 lb of raw peeled shrimp

1/2 lb of raw cleaned squid (tubes and tentacles)

3/4 lb of raw octopus tentacles

24 raw clams washed

24 raw mussels washed

1/2 cup of red onions cut finely sliced vertically from top to bottom -émincé style- (yellow or white onions work as substitute)

1/2 cup of yellow bell pepper finely sliced (any color bell pepper work as substitute)

1/2 cup of diced celery

6 garlic cloves finely minced

2 Tbsp. of minced fresh parsley (fresh cilantro works as substitute)

1/2 cup of extra virgin olive oil

3 limes (lemons work as substitute)

2 tsp. of hot sauce (optional)

Salt

Ground black pepper (ground white pepper works as substitute)

Preparation

1 In a medium pot over medium heat, put 4 cups of water and bring it to a boil. Add the octopus and 1 tsp. of salt, bring back to a boil, cover it and cook for 45 minutes. Take out the octopus from the boiling water and submerge it in a bowl with enough water with ice. Once the octopus is cold, cut the tentacles in 1/2'' slices, put them on a dry container and keep it in the fridge. Reserve the stock where the octopus has been cooked so you can use it in other recipes.

2 Cut the clean squid tubes in 1/2'' rings, cut the heads with tentacles in halves and reserve. Cut the shrimp in halves (leave them whole if they are small). In a medium pot over medium heat, put 3 cups of water and bring it to a boil. Add 1 tsp. of salt and add the squid and shrimp pieces, let it boil again and cook for 3 minutes. Take the pieces of shrimp and squid out with a slotted spoon and submerge them in a bowl with enough water with ice. Once they are cold, put them in a dry container and keep it in the fridge.

3 In the same pot with the remaining of the water used to cook the shrimp and the squid, bring the stock back to a boil and place inside the mussels and clams. Cook them until they open, which would happen about 1 minute after it starts boiling again. Discard any that doesn´t open, that means they are not good for consumption. Take the remaining shellfish out of the boiling stock with a slotted spoon and place them in a container, let them cool for 5 minutes, take the flesh out of the shells and put them in a small container and keep it in the fridge. Reserve the stock where the seafood has been cooked and use it for other recipes.

4 In a large bowl place the octopus, shrimp and squid pieces, add the mussels and clams' flesh, the onions, celery, parsley and bell peppers. Add 1/2 tsp. of salt and 1/2 tsp. of ground black pepper. Squeeze the limes on top of everything, add the hot sauce and extra virgin olive oil. Mix everything and make sure that all the ingredients are incorporated well to create an even flavor profile in the salad. Taste it and add more salt, pepper and hot sauce if needed. Keep it cold inside the fridge until serving. Enjoy!

SALMON TARTARE

You will notice a really big difference making this delicious dish with wild caught salmon instead of farmed salmon. For us it is a delight when we get wild Alaskan salmon, brings back the memories of an amazing trip we made all the way up to the Artic Circle!

4 PORTIONS **55** min PREP TIME **0** min COOKING TIME

Preparation

1 Cut the salmon fillets in dices of 1/4'. Put them in a bowl, add and mix 1 tsp. of salt and 1 tsp. of ground black pepper.

2 Add the diced bell peppers, diced onions, spring onions, capers, hot sauce, dill, chives and ginger. Squeeze the limes and add the extra virgin olive oil on top. Mix everything together well, to create an even flavor profile. Taste the tartare and add more salt and ground pepper if needed. Cover the bowl with a plastic saran wrap, put it in the fridge and let it sit for at least 30 minutes. (You can use an airtight container instead). Enjoy!

Ingredients

1.5 lb of wild caught salmon fillets skinned and boned (farmed salmon works as substitute)

1 cup of finely diced red bell pepper (any color bell pepper works as substitute)

1 cup of finely diced red onions (yellow or white onions work as substitute)

1/4 cup of finely sliced spring onions

4 Tbsp. of capers

2 tsp. of hot sauce (optional)

2 Tbsp. of minced fresh dill (dry dill works as substitute)

2 Tbsp. of minced chives (dry chives work as substitute)

4 Tbsp. of extra virgin olive oil

2 limes (lemons work as substitute)

2 tsp. of ground ginger

Salt

Ground black pepper (ground white pepper works as substitute)

FISH TACOS

I have a strong belief that in one of my previous lives I was Mexican, I really love their food. Paul and I enjoyed a lot our trip to Cancun, particularly to the ruins of Tulum. This colorful and tasty recipe brings those memories back to us!

Ingredients

1 lb of white fish skinned fillets (sea bass, grouper, snapper or cod)

1 cup of shredded white cabbage

1/3 cup of shredded purple cabbage

1/4 cup of shredded carrots

3 radishes thinly sliced

12 corn tortillas for tacos (wheat tortillas work as substitute)

1 cup of all-purpose flour

1 cup of chicken stock (beef stock or vegetable stock works as substitute)

1/2 tsp. of baking powder

2 Tbsp. of minced fresh cilantro (dry cilantro works as substitute)

1 Tbsp. of minced spring onions

1 tsp. of spicy paprika (sweet paprika works as substitute)

4 Tbsp. of sour cream

1 Tbsp. of mayonnaise

1 lime (lemon works as substitute)

1 Tbsp. of hot sauce (optional)

2 minced garlic cloves

1 ripe hass avocado

Corn oil (other vegetable oil works as substitute, except olive oil)

Salt

Ground white pepper (Ground black pepper works as substitute)

Preparation

1 Cut the fish fillets in pieces of about 2"x1/2"x1/2". Salt and pepper them and reserve in a bowl on the side.

2 In a large bowl put the all-purpose flour, baking powder, spicy paprika, cilantro, spring onions and chicken stock. Mix all the ingredients well until create a homogeneous batter. Let it sit for 10 minutes.

3 In another bowl mix the white cabbage, purple cabbage and carrots, toss it well to create the cabbage slaw. In another small bowl mix the sour cream, mayonnaise, minced garlic, hot sauce, 1/2 tsp. of salt, 1/2 tsp. of ground white pepper, squeeze 1 lime on top of everything and mix well to create the seasoning white sauce to top the tacos.

4 In a deep fry pan over medium heat, put the corn oil (or other vegetable oil different than olive oil) enough to fill the pan around 3/4 of its capacity. Let the oil heat for 4 minutes. Coat 4 or 5 pieces of fish with the batter and fry them in the oil for 5 minutes, flip them with a slotted spoon from time to time until golden. Take them out of the oil and place them in a large bowl covered with paper towels. Repeat this process for all the fish pieces.

5 Pit the avocado by making a cut with a chef knife lengthwise all around it. Twist each half of the avocado in an opposite direction with your hands and separate them. Take out the pit of the half that still have it by sticking the knife edge lengthwise and twist it, the pit should stick to the knife. Using a metal spoon separate the flesh out of the skin of each half of the avocado and put them over a cutting board. Cut 6 slices of each half to make a total of 12.

6 Heat the tortillas in a cast iron grill or in the oven or in the microwave. Place them in a plate or in a taco base, put a bit of the cabbage slaw on top of them, then two or three pieces of fried fish and two or three radish slices, cover with the seasoning white sauce. Garnish with fresh cilantro leaves and a slice of avocado on each taco. Enjoy!

DESSERTS

"I think life is about falling in love with the right person,
shopping, eating our favorite desserts
and traveling a lot"

Olivia Palermo - 2013

AMANDA'S PINEAPPLE QUESILLO

This recipe is very close to my heart.
Even though my beloved Amanda Sanchez taught me how to make this delicious dessert, I will never make it as good as hers. I believe that her unconditional loving is the secret ingredient I am missing every time I make it. Nevertheless, it is an outstanding example of our traditional Venezuelan desserts. Keep taking good care of us from heaven my dearest Amanda, love you and miss you every day!

16
PORTIONS

2hrs + overnight cooling
PREP TIME

2hrs
COOKING TIME

Ingredients

1 pineapple of approx. 2 lb
(whole chunks of peeled pineapple
work as substitute)

12 eggs

4 cups of sugar

1 tsp. of vanilla extract

For the caramel

1 cup of sugar

1/2 cup of water

Preparation

1 Peel the pineapple and cut it in quarts. In large bowl place a clean kitchen cloth covering the bottom of it. Grate a pineapple quart using the coarser holes of the grater on top of the kitchen cloth. Squeeze the grated pineapple twisting the kitchen cloth to obtain the juice. Repeat this process with all the pineapple quarts. This should obtain 4 cups of juice approximately.

2 In a medium pot over medium-low level heat, place the pineapple juice and the 4 cups of sugar, stir until dissolve. Bring this to a boil and let it cook uncovered for 40 minutes, stirring every 10 minutes. Turn off the heat and let the pineapple sirup cool for at least 1 hour.

3 In a small pot over low level heat put 1 cup of sugar and 1/2 cup of water, stir until dissolve. Bring it to a boil and let it cook for about 10 to 12 minutes, until the caramel browns but avoid burning it. Cover the bottom of a 9''x3'' cake pan with the caramel, twisting it around so an even layer covers it. Let it cool.

4 In a blender with a large vase, crack the 12 eggs and blend at high speed for 1 minute. Add the vanilla extract and add slowly the pineapple sirup while still blending, once all the sirup has been added, blend for an extra 30 seconds and turn it off. (If your blender vase is not large enough, you can divide the ingredients in half for this step and make it twice).

5 Put the blended ingredients in the cake pan with the previously caramelized bottom, cover the bake pan with aluminum foil making sure it is tightly covered. Put it in the middle of a 15″×10″ tempered glass (Pyrex) baking dish and add water to the container until it covers at least half of the bake pan height. Bake in the oven at 350° F for 2 hours.
To make sure the quesillo is done, uncover the bake pan and pinch it with a butter knife, if it comes out clean or almost clean, it's done.

6 Take the bake pan out of the hot water bath and let it cool for 1 hour. Put it in the fridge and let it cool overnight. Take it out of the fridge at least 30 minutes before demolding, use a butter knife to separate the quesillo from the walls of the pan, place a large plate (10″ or larger) on top it, flip it quickly and tap on top of the pan, lift it and let the caramel cover the bottom of the plate. Serve and enjoy!

TRES LECHES

Someone once said to us that this Tres Leches was "better than sex!" Although we won't affirm this, nor deny it, this is an amazing dessert that is worth it to make, share and enjoy. This is my mom's recipe, who I love and miss every day. I am very proud to share it with you, so you can become part of our family.

12 PORTIONS **45**min + overnight cooling PREP TIME **35**min COOKING TIME

Ingredients

4 eggs

3/4 cup of sugar

3/4 cup of all-purpose flour

1/2 tsp. of baking powder

2 tsp. of vanilla extract

1 lime zest

1 can of 14 oz of condensed milk

1 can of 12 oz of evaporated milk

12 oz of heavy cream

2 Tbsp. of rum (optional)

1/8 tsp. of salt

For the merengue topping

4 egg whites

14 Tbsp. of sugar

1 lime zest

Preparation

1 Separate the whites from the yolks of 4 eggs, put the egg whites in a big bowl. Beat them with a hand mixer at high speed until stand in soft peaks, add the yolks one by one until all is well mixed. Continue beating and add little by little the sugar, add 1 tbs. of vanilla extract and 1 lime zest.

2 In a medium bowl, sift the flour, baking powder and salt. Add this dry mix slowly to the wet ingredients and keep beating with the hand mixer at the lowest speed, just to incorporate them to the batter, avoid over mixing it.

3 Grease and flour a 9''x9'' baking pan. Put the battered mix in the baking pan, and place it in the oven at 350° F for 30 to 35 minutes. Check if it is ready by inserting a butter knife in the middle of the sponge cake, if it comes out clean it is ready.

4 When the sponge cake is 5 minutes to be ready, make the Tres Leches Bath: put in a blender vase the condensed milk, evaporated milk and heavy cream and 1 tsp. of vanilla extract. Blend for 1 minute, add the rum and keep blending for another minute. When the sponge cake is ready, remove from the oven and add the Tres Leches Bath on top of it while the cake is still hot. Let it cool to room temperature, cover the baking pan with aluminum foil and put it in the fridge overnight.

5 Make the merengue the next day. Put 4 egg whites in a medium bowl and beat them with a hand mixer at high speed until stand in soft peaks. Add 14 tablespoons of sugar one by one in intervals of 30 seconds, while still mixing at high speed. Add 1 lime zest and mix it for 30 seconds more to incorporate it well.

6 Take the baking pan out of the fridge, put on top of it the merengue creating an even and thick layer. You can create peaks or shapes with it, brown them with a torch or the oven broil, you can also decorate with lime zest, caramel or sliced almonds. Use your creativity and imagination! Enjoy!

www.ingramcontent.com/pod-product-compliance
Lightning Source LLC
Chambersburg PA
CBHW042014080426
42735CB00002B/51